Sound Me When I'm Done

Sound Me When I'm Done

edited
by
Lorna Crozier

WINTERGREEN
STUDIOS PRESS

Wintergreen Studios Press
Township of South Frontenac
PO Box 75, Yarker, ON, Canada K0K 3N0

Book and cover design by Rena Upitis
Edited by Lorna Crozier and Susan Alexander
Front artwork: Ink drawing by Melanie Craig-Hansford

Composed in Book Antiqua and Candara, typefaces designed by Monotype Typography and Gary Munch, respectively.

Library and Archives Canada Cataloguing in Publication
Crozier, Lorna.
Sound Me When I'm Done/Lorna Crozier
ISBN: 978-0-9918722-5-1
1.
Poetry — General.
I. Title. Sound Me When I'm Done.
Legal Deposit — Library and Archives Canada

Contents

Poetry and Wintergreen

Poetry is the most solitary and life-enriching genre. It leads both writer and reader to that "small open place," where memory arrives on a scent, a whisper, a "small mauve blossom on the tongue." Sometimes it arrives with the tastes of "almond, of vinegar and ash."

You have to trust the poem when it comes to you on the page; you have to "swing for [your] life and let go." You have to say to yourself as the lines unfold, "Now you have what matters."

When you open yourself to the music of words, it's as if the skull, a "choreography of bone," guides you in the dance. Like the body, the poem "struggles to find balance" between the awkward and the smooth, between sound and meaning, between excess and restraint.

Wintergreen, with grace and compassion, provides the space, the stillness, the care that nudges our best selves, our most creative selves, into being. It is a magical studio where the inspired and the imaginative thrive. As we walk its pathways, we're reminded that, "we live under stars." In such a place we hear not only each other but also "the earth's bone…what it's been shouting all these years." And in such rare moments, off the grid of our urban lives, we get the sense that "the wild is coming back in."

Those who took part in our retreat were able to "spin magic cloth from the web of language," to carry into the darkness a blazing light that "lets us enter" places we were afraid to go. The poetry written in our short time together tells a "truth that knocks you over." Though the heart is speechless, on the pages of this book, "it thrums a message"; it "answers [our] not knowing."

One morning, I asked each of the participants to write about silence, and then I constructed from their images and sensibilities a poem. The mix of their voices is perhaps the best introduction to this collection.

Lorna Crozier
June 2016

Sound Me When I'm Done

The distant death of thunder, now
snow on snow. The reverence of
that moment like a beach stone, unique
perfect, complete. Sometimes your silence
is deafening. The owl's round note
rises, rises again and falls.
Dust settles into the night fields.
Who is gathered around me
as I make this bed? Is there a horror
that can't be spoken? The silence that lives
in a dark house when love dies.
In this absence, there's too much of me.
I will listen to the single blade of grass,
the blue-spotted salamander that breathes
through his skin. Sound me when I'm done.
There's a deeper silence I cannot enter yet.

SUSAN WISMER

The Babysitter

When I was four I wanted to touch
Mrs. Lees' throat
my small hand poised, delicate
in the warm air close
to her, tracing

the cup of her bone, the beautiful notch
at the base of her neck,
the rounded line of her plain
navy blue dress.
She didn't mind.

On those happy rare evenings
when our parents went out,
in my place on her lap,
its comforts, its warmth,
a whisper of perfume, smells of
flowers and play,

I could see clearly her moonbeam-pale skin,
a tiny brush painting, a sketching of folds
held in her hollow, soft skin rimming bone.
How her skin fluttered softly
with each beat of her heart.

By the time I was six, I knew
what everyone knew in our small town —
husband long gone, drunkard son
still at home with her in
a little apartment over the ladies' wear shop.
She sat children evenings
making ends meet.

I choose to believe, she went to the drugstore,
bought Evening in Paris
opened up the blue bottle
right there in the store

touched a warm worn finger
firm and fragrant, to that small open place where
my child's hand had lingered.

Walked, proudly and kindly,
home through the town
in old shoes, her one blue dress.

6

SUSAN WHELEHAN

For My Life

Shirtless, strong, smiling
you hold out your hand.
Shimmering in sequins, I take it.
You whisper *I will catch you.*
We walk to my ladder
hanging from the tent ceiling.
I climb to the platform and wait.
I swallow my last spit and smile.
My lips stick to my teeth.
You climb your ladder,
grab the trapeze and launch yourself into the air.

                                Towards me —

and back.

                                Towards me —

and back.

            Now you hang

                        by

                        your

                        knees.

                                Towards me —
and back.

                        I swing for my life —

                            and let

                                go

CAROL A. STEPHEN

What Rises on the Tongue

The heart from its great distance watches, helpless,
thrums a steady thrub-dup bongo, as the bloodstream
hums in tune. This rhythmic drum, this body-beat
knows no jazz riff to syncopate a troubled mind.

The heart, too far, is helpless
to stop the flow of bitter juice
that rises on the tongue
in words that taste of almond, vinegar and ash.

The first line of this poem is based on the last line of Jane Hirshfield's
poem *Red Onion, Cherries, Boiling Potatoes, Milk.*

RONA SHAFFRAN

The Skull

In memoriam

It's a cradle
a playpen
a sandbox
a pine cabin
a white wicker basket
a weekly pill box
a four-wheel walker
a bleached coffin

The skull, choreography
of bone, nest of soul
walled city for the living
empty house for the dead
eternal companion

ELIZABETH PAULETTE-COUGHLIN

Lilacs

I am fading into lilac, now,
fading into my pastel self,
remembering a springtime long ago.

Lilacs, too high for a child to reach.
My father holds the ladder, as I climb
that stairway to the sky.

My five-year-old face in lilacs.

When I think of him now,
I smell their jasmine honey.

In the graveyard, the lilacs grow.

Beside the fence
covered with lichen,
        a rusty half-opened gate,

black granite,

his name etched in stone.

I put the small mauve blossom
on my tongue,
        a remedy to forgetting.

RUTH MCKINNEY

In Which The Poet Apologizes To Her Feet

My mother loved my chubby newborn feet,
anointing them each morning with Johnson's baby oil,
first counting the toes, and then the days
to my first steps. My struggle
to find balance, and then, motion,
a marker she recorded
in my baby book.

First Sensations — ticklish feet,
cool grass beneath bare skin,
the itch of sand between my toes.

Feet — you walked me to school and down the aisle,
and took me dancing in the middle of the day,
never questioning the commands
of muscles and brain.

The knees, the hips, complained,
begging for physio — or perhaps even —
replacement.

I gave you little thought, and
less attention.
Why did I start taking you for granted?

Tonight I'll warm you with sesame oil,
wrap you in fleece.
Tomorrow, as I swing my legs from the bed,
you will be the first thing on my mind.

JULIA MCARTHUR

Return to Nature

Cottage carved out of the wildwood,
A few trees cleared
For a view of the lake.
Some grass for the septic tank,
A lane to drive out to the road,
For a waterfront retreat.

But farmers have given up trying to farm
This raped and drowned landscape.
Now deer graze in overgrown fields,
Bears harvest acorns in the fall,
We hear the wolves howl at night.

It's fairy tale time,
The wild is coming back in.

CALLISTA MARKOTICH

Cut to the Purple Sage

The *ocotillos* must be sacrificed.
Heap the thorny tinder upon the scorched trail;
Let the flaming blossoms ignite within the pyre.
Herd the javelina, chuffing crossly, away
On peccary tiptoes, hide them in a stand of willows.

Horses? They must go, the bay, the paint, the grullo.
Have those black-eyed children lead them them away,
Across the pale sand. Let them splash
Shank-deep in the *arroyo*.
No adobe huts crumbling, no hawk slides across the blue.

No *vaqueros*, driving dusty longhorns,
Look, they are decamping now, they ride
Into the inky cordillera: they've seen the lay of the land;
Serapes flapping, now they stand in their stirrups and turn
To shoot, or to shout, *Adios!* Cut to the purple sage.

What you have left is your father,
In a chair with his Zane Grey,
After a day at a branch of The Bank Of Nova Scotia.
Now you have what matters.
Look. He will turn over his book and smile.

Zane Grey was a writer of Western classics, whose most well known novel
is *Riders of the Purple Sage*.

ROSEMARIE KRAUSZ

Into the Dance

it's the one with the green-eyed gaze
who charms me like chocolate

his mind   a flying trapeze that scoops
me up and spins me dizzy

turned on by his forearms   (it's my fetish—
like chicken drumsticks I could bite into)
I let him lead me down   down
down into the mountain cave   his flashlight

lapping over the ancient scrawls
but my eyes embrace only his form—

taut   and lithe   and perfect—
as he descends into the womblike core

(I had been here too   once, long ago
terror-stricken in my nightmare then)

the air is a trill of clarinet
the ground pungent with mushrooms

and he begins to speak—
once—he says—once before

I came here and learned how to live
and now — I want to share with you

how the darkness lets us enter
into the dance   and when it ends

we will not leave
but sleep   like bears in winter

SUSAN HALDANE

Anthropology of Alien Funeral Customs

We do not
cushion our dead in satin with a wooden shell
and stock them in grids
underground.

We do not introduce them to fire.

We do not crepe black the mirrors
to ease the dead's escape.

We do not transfuse fluids or paint
skin, or proceed
slowly in black lines.

We do not rock the dead in boats
on salt rivers.

Here, we let them be the mirror, the one
by the door where you finger your hair,
leaving.

We let them be the flame.

We take them in our hands, the dead, warm
and mould them
and give them to the sky.

We live under stars, here.

JANICE FALLS

Then There Were Poems

In my childhood, there were always stories
and then there were poems,
teaching me how to make word pictures.
Feeling invisible, almost wordless,
I depended on the words of others to find me,
to describe the shimmering images,
the ephemeral feelings that lay under my tongue.

I longed to be the fairy tale goose girl
who spun magic cloth from the web of language,
weaving words into poetry
but that elusive beauty stayed locked within.
Still, I gathered the bright jewels of words,
playing with their patterns.
loving their sound in my ears,
their feel in my mouth when I spoke.

Line by line, poetry gave me visibility
until a voice of my own emerged,
tangled, awkward, stuttering.
Then I practiced, over and over,
like learning a new language, a new song
and poems sang me into being.

MELANIE CRAIG-HANSFORD

Finding My Voice

I can't write another fucking poem about a tree. I tried to ponder the perfection of the poplar. I wrote drivel about walks in the woods and read so many Mary Oliver poems I could spit. Nature will be gone soon and then who will be my muse? I want to write wild anecdotes about sex and cooking shows and sex with chefs on cooking shows. Or maybe a poem about having sex in a maple tree and doing erotic things with maple syrup; or how wood chips feels on bare feet after stumbling outside, after drinking too much scotch.

I can't write another fucking poem about a tree. I want to be the kind of poet who tells the truth about how gratitude sometimes seems overrated or how parenting is so hard it makes you want to stick twigs in your eyes or how I climbed the oak in our back yard so I could scream away my frustration at a world that wants me to be a woman in high heels when all I want to wear is Merino wool socks and Birks … at the same time.

I can't write another fucking poem about a tree so I will sit under one, instead, and tell tales of bonfires gone bad, of my scars from roasted marshmallow fights and a world where truth knocks you over with brilliant hyperbole not hidden behind lame metaphors about lovely walks in the woods.

MARY CORKERY

The Other Side

House flooded with silence,
          her heart heaves, thrusts
flutters upstairs to his bedroom door where it hovers
red sac pumping
above a door closed for hours.

Speechless, heart thrums a message
he can't hear through a thickening cloud
of grief seeping down the hall, its acrid
smell. Leaving heart on guard
she rushes downstairs to do what she must —

put on the kettle. On the teak tray
she sets earl grey, last slice
of carrot cake, lays it at the foot of his door,
raps her knuckles raw
until the door opens, just a crack.

As her fifteen-year-old son
edges toward the tray, she seizes
this opening, to hug

          while the heart, from its distance, glimpses
the other side —
a boy's tender heart, broken
          by a charming, erratic girl.
          She didn't know
it happened to boys.

SANDRA CAMPBELL

Soon, you too will be silent, the poet says

For Alan

Tongues under silence

Come to me

Twirl inside my ears

Wrap yourselves around my lobes

Language me.

Tell me my question

Answer my not knowing

Suck me into mystery

Will you sound me when I'm done?

SUSAN ALEXANDER

There

She climbs the tree of knowledge
and the tree of life that grow there —
wild orchards of them
beyond the old broken walls.
Fruit for every living creature.
Everbearing.

The fruit of knowledge is juicy,
soft as peach. Life,
more citrus with a thicker peel,
a different taste
according to the season.

She sits still
among columbines
those petalled rockets of fire.
She listens to earth's bone
Precambrian stone
and begins to hear
what it's been shouting
all these years.

Contributors

Susan Wismer is a poet, a gardener, a grandmother, a dancer. She lives gratefully nestled by the shores of Georgian Bay in Collingwood, Ontario.

Susan Whelehan lives in Toronto with her husband, Francis Corrigan. With Anne Laurel Carter, Susie co-edited and contributed to "My Wedding Dress: True-Life Tales of Lace, Laughter, Tears and Tulle," Vintage Canada. That's how she met Lorna and Sandra! She's hoping to collaborate (or anything, really) with Bruce Springsteen someday.

Carol A. Stephen is a Carleton Place poet, and Ottawa Manager for The Ontario Poetry Society. She is a former member of CAA-NCR and Tree Reading Series boards. Her poetry has won awards or been shortlisted in CAA's National Capital Writing Contest and has appeared in anthologies, journals, and online. Carol has authored three chapbooks and co-authored two chapbooks of collaborative poems.

Rona Shaffran co-directs RailRoad, Ottawa's pop-up poetry reading series. Signature Editions published Rona's *Ignite* in 2013. A graduate of Humber's School for Writers and the Banff Centre's Writing Studio, Rona has read her poems at literary festivals and reading series across Canada. She is at work on a prose novella.

Elizabeth Paulette-Coughlin is the lover of a lake so deep it is almost bottomless. If you want to find me in summer, look in the water. If I'm not there, try the cedar groves. I may be lying belly-down on the cool dark earth. When not in these places, I'll be walking my own camino, the dirt road travelled by my ancestors.

Ruth McKinney is a poet living in Kingston, Ontario. A poetry junkie, she has been writing — for love or money — all her life and is thrilled to finally be able to do it just for love.

Julia McArthur is an artist and art historian living in Kingston. Having thought of herself as a largely visual person, she was surprised to realize at Wintergreen how much of her life has been informed by the music of poetry: from R. L. Stevenson to Leigh Hunt, Amy Lowell, Pablo Neruda, and even Ernest Hemingway.

Callista Markotich was a Teacher, Principal, and Superintendent of Education, who, in that capacity has written hundreds of reports, memos and letters, and celebrates the power of the written word to inform, influence, request, and thank. At Wintergreen, with Lorna and the other poets, Callie fully enjoyed a deep immersion in the most exquisite of forms, Poetry.

Rosemarie Krausz is a retired psychologist and psycho-analyst who has been writing poetry for the last three years. For her, writing poetry is a natural extension of self-analysis. She is working on a collection of poems about her childhood with parents who were Holocaust survivors. She lives in Manotick, Ontario.

Susan Haldane lives and writes in Northern Ontario, where she and her husband operate a farm. Her work has previously been published in *Room*, *The New Quarterly* and in the anthology *Desperately Seeking Susans*.

Janice Falls is an English literature graduate and a psychotherapist, now semi-retired to pursue her love of reading, writing and speaking poetry. She studies with Kim Rosen (*Saved by a Poem*) and has attended workshops with Ellen Bass and Lorna Crozier. She works and learns with an online writing group.

Melanie Craig-Hansford graduated from The Nova Scotia College of Art and Design in 1985 with a Bachelor of Fine Art and Arts Education. She has recently retired from teaching high school in Kingston, Ontario. Melanie now lives in Erbs Cove, New Brunswick where she is committed to living a creative life filled with poetry and art. Melanie co-wrote a book called *Prayers for Women Who Can't Pray* published by Wintergreen Studios Press. This is her second chapbook contribution. Her drawing appears on the cover.

Mary Corkery worked many decades for social justice and international development. Now retired, she writes poetry, which has been published in journals in Canada, USA, and the UK. Her poetry book, *Simultaneous Windows*, will be published by Inanna, spring 2017. Mary lives in Toronto with her husband, Ted Hyland.

Sandra Campbell writes fiction and non-fiction and has tried her hand at a few docs. In the last few years she has fallen deeply in love with poetry. She treasures her retreats at Wintergreen with Lorna who opens her to listening to the deepest chords of her being.

Susan Alexander is grateful for another spring week of trilliums, poets, columbines, scribbling, violets, calls, responses and beaver dams at Wintergreen Studios. What a delight to be well fed — in every sense and in every sense of the word. Thank you Lorna for again generously sharing your talent and time with us.

Wintergreen Studios Press is an independent literary press. It is affiliated with the not-for-profit educational retreat centre, Wintergreen Studios, and supports the work of Wintergreen Studios by publishing works related to education, the arts, and the environment.

www.wintergreenstudios.com

WINTERGREEN
STUDIOS PRESS